SYLLABUS STANDARD 9

YEARLY PLANNER FOR ACADEMIC YEAR 2022-23

AASHISH

To all the dedicated learners and parents.

Contents

Foreword

I believe that education shapes the character, calibre and prospect of an individual. Education has no perimeter to restrict. Intensive and critical thinking, sharpening intelligence, refining character —all are a part of dignified education. Students of Heavenly Blessings Academy are benefitted by such type of education.

Preface

This book contains complete syllabus for Class 8 CBSE for the subjects of English, Mathematics, Science and Social Science. It also contains paper patterns and Marks wise weightage for every lesson of all the subjects.

Yearly planner is also mentioned at last.

Few additional activities that will be conducted this year: I-IBPL Season 3: Box Cricket Tournament.

Movie Time.

Trek Trip: If things go well with permissions.

Academic Competitions: Elocution, Debate, *etc.*

Book Writing Activity.

This year we would also provide extra books 'FIB Spotlight' that will contain summarised lessons in lucid language, solutions to INERT Textual Questions, Extra Important Mark wise Questions, Important MC Q and lots more.

Why to select us?

Because all the costs are included in the fees and no extra cost will be

incurred! Neither for the Andriod Application or for the Extra Books, Activities, Tests, Trips, Practicals, ID cards, etc. etc. etc.

Acknowledgements

Special Thanks to my team of learners, motivators, friends, parents and Team Heavenly Blessings.

Prologue

My Goals This Year:

I will help to create a shared vision for students, staff and community members. I will take the time to gather input and knowledge from as many stakeholders as possible.

I will utilize my supervisory time to build and establish relationships with students and staff.

I will talk with students and staff and ask them about their lives in a sincere and caring manner.

I will take an active interest in learning as much as I can about them.

I will have high expectations for students, staff and myself.

I will help to empower others to take control of their own learning and development by establishing an environment built on accountability and responsibility.

I will support and encourage those with whom I work.

I will work to embrace a sharing and collaborative school culture that takes risks in an effort to do great things.

I will listen more than I talk.

I will use my two ears more than I use my one mouth, and I will try to learn as much as I can from others.

I will make it a priority to get into classrooms to observe on a daily basis, and I will learn by listening and observing.

I will communicate with and involve parents and community stakeholders as often as possible.

I will work with teachers and staff to keep parents informed and up-to-date with what is going on in our school through the use of weekly newsletters, our school website and social media outlets.

I will share the power of my PLN with my colleagues. I will take the time to meet with anyone interested in learning more about using social media as a means toward professional growth.

I will model being a lifelong learner for both students and staff.

I will have a healthy balance between my professional and personal life.

Though I anticipate the high level of time commitment required for this job, I do not want my job to consume my entire life. My family, friends and colleagues will all benefit from this healthy balance. I will base every decision I make on what is best for students. It is difficult to not get caught up in everything that is going on, but I will make every effort to put students and their needs first.

CHAPTER ONE

English Syllabus Term I

Course Structure for CBSE Class 9 English (Code No. 184) 2021-2022 (Term I):

SECTION	WEIGHTAGE (IN MARKS)
READING	10
WRITING & GRAMMAR	10
LITERATURE	20
TOTAL	40
INTERNAL ASSESSMENT	10
GRAND TOTAL	50

Pattern for Term 1 and Term 2

Reading-

Question based on the following kinds of unseen passages to assess inference, evaluation, vocabulary, analysis and interpretation:

1. Discursive passage (400-450 words)

2. Case based Factual passage (with visual input/ statistical data/ chart etc. 200-250 words)

Writing-

1. Descriptive paragraph (Person)

2. Short Story (based on beginning line, outline, cues etc.)

Grammar-

1. Tenses

2. Subject-Verb Concord

3. Modals

4. Determiners

5. Reported Speech

6. Commands and Requests

7. Statements

8. Questions

Literature

Questions based on extracts /texts to assess interpretation, inference, extrapolation beyond the text and across the texts.

Moments

1. The Lost Child

2. The Adventures of Toto

3. In the Kingdom of Fools

4. The Happy Prince

Beehive

Prose

1. The Fun They Had

2. The Sound of Music

3. The Little Girl

4. A Truly Beautiful Mind

5. My Childhood

Poems

1. The Road Not Taken

2. Wind

3. Rain on The Roof

4. A Legend of The Northland

Mathematics Syllabus Term I

COURSE STRUCTURE CLASS –IX (2021-22) FIRST TERM

Unit No.	Unit Name	Marks
I	NUMBER SYSTEMS	8
II	ALGEBRA	5
III	COORDINATE GEOMETRY	4
IV	GEOMETRY	13
V	MENSURATION	4
VI	STATISTICS & PROBABILITY	6
	Total	40
	INTERNAL ASSESSMENT	10
	TOTAL	50

Pattern For Term 1

UNIT- NUMBER SYSTEMS

1. NUMBER SYSTEM

Review of representation of natural numbers, integers, rational numbers on the number line. Rational numbers as recurring/ terminating decimals. Operations on real numbers.

1. Examples of non-recurring/non-terminating decimals. Existence of non-rational numbers (irrational numbers) such as $\sqrt{2}, \sqrt{3}$ and their representation on the number

2. Rationalization (with precise meaning) of real numbers of the type $1/(?+?\sqrt{?})$ and $1/(\sqrt{?}+\sqrt{?})$ (and their combinations) where x and y are natural number and a and b are integers.

3. Recall of laws of exponents with integral powers. Rational exponents with positive real bases (to be done by particular cases, allowing learner to arrive at the general laws.)

UNIT-ALGEBRA

2. LINEAR EQUATIONS IN TWO VARIABLES

Recall of linear equations in one variable. Introduction to the equation in two variables. Focus on linear equations of the type ax + by + c=0.

Explain that a linear equation in two variables has infinitely many solutions and justify their being written as ordered pairs of real numbers, plotting them and showing that they lie on a line.

Graph of linear equations in two variables.

Examples, problems from real life with algebraic and graphical solutions being done simultaneously

UNIT-COORDINATE GEOMETRY

3. COORDINATE GEOMETRY

The Cartesian plane, coordinates of a point, names and terms associated with the coordinate plane, notations, plotting points in the plane.

UNIT-GEOMETRY

4. LINES AND ANGLES

1. (Motivate) If a ray stands on a line, then the sum of the two adjacent angles so formed is 180° and the converse.

2. (Prove) If two lines intersect, vertically opposite angles are equal.

3. (Motivate) Results on corresponding angles, alternate angles, interior angles when a transversal intersects two parallel lines.

4. (Motivate) Lines which are parallel to a given line are parallel.

5. (Prove) The sum of the angles of a triangle is 180°.

6. (Motivate) If a side of a triangle is produced, the exterior angle so formed is equal to the sum of the two interior opposite angles.

5. TRIANGLES

1. (Motivate) Two triangles are congruent if any two sides and the included angle of one triangle is equal to any two sides and the included angle of the other triangle (SAS Congruence).

2. (Motivate) Two triangles are congruent if any two angles and the included side of one triangle is equal to any two angles and the included side of the other triangle (ASA Congruence).

3. (Motivate) Two triangles are congruent if the three sides of one triangle are equal to three sides of the other triangle (SSS Congruence).

4. (Motivate) Two right triangles are congruent if the hypotenuse and a side of one triangle are equal (respectively) to the hypotenuse and a side of the other triangle. (RHS Congruence)

5. (Prove) The angles opposite to equal sides of a triangle are equal.

6. (Motivate) The sides opposite to equal angles of a triangle are equal.

7. (Motivate) The sides opposite to equal angles of a triangle are equal.

UNIT-MENSURATION

6. HERON'S FORMULA

Area of a triangle using Heron's formula (without proof)

UNIT-STATISTICS & PROBABILITY

7. STATISTICS

Introduction to Statistics: Collection of data, presentation of data — tabular form, ungrouped / grouped, bar graphs, histograms

Internal Assessment (IA) for Term 1

Components of IA	Marks	Total Marks
Periodic Tests 3	3	
Multiple Assessments	2	
		10
Portfolio	2	
Student Enrichment Activities-practical work	3	

Internal Assessment Term 1

For Mathematics, students will also be provided with NCERT Exemplar for prescribed extra questions practices.

CHAPTER THREE

Science Syllabus Term I

CBSE Class 9 Science (Subject Code - 086) Syllabus 2021-22 (Term 1)

General Instructions:

1. The total Theory Examinations (Term I+II) will be of 80 marks and 20 marks weightage shall be for Internal Assessment (Term I+II).

2. Internal Assessment - Maximum Marks 10 for each Term:

a. There will be Periodic Assessment that would include:

Three periodic tests will be conducted by the school in the entire session. The average of the two periodic tests/marks of the best periodic test conducted in the Term is to be taken into consideration.

Diverse methods of assessment as per the need of the class dynamics and curriculum transaction. These may include - short tests, oral test, quiz, concept maps, projects, posters, presentations, enquiry based scientific investigations, etc.

b. Subject Enrichment in the form of Practical/Laboratory work should be done throughout the year and the student should maintain record of the same. Practical Assessment should be continuous. All practicals listed in the syllabus must be completed.

c. Portfolio to be prepared by the student- This would include classwork and other sample of student work.

Units	Term-I	Marks
I	Matter-Its Nature and Behaviour: Chapter - 2	09
II	Organization in the Living World: Chapter - 5 and 6	18
III	Motion, Force and Work: Chapter - 8 and 9	13
	Total	40
	Internal Assessment	10
	Total	50

Assessment Pattern Term I

Theme: Materials
Unit I: Matter- It's Nature and Behaviour

Chapter – 2 Is matter around us Pure

Nature of matter: Elements, compounds and mixtures. Heterogeneous and homogenous mixtures, colloids and suspensions.

Theme: The World of the Living
Unit II: Organization in the Living World

Chapter – 5 The Fundamental Unit of Life

Cell - Basic Unit of life: Cell as a basic unit of life; prokaryotic and eukaryotic cells, multicellular organisms; cell membrane and cell wall, cell organelles and cell inclusions; chloroplast, mitochondria, vacuoles, endoplasmic reticulum, Golgi apparatus; nucleus, chromosomes - basic structure, number.

Chapter – 6 Tissues

Tissues, Organs, Organ System, Organism: Structure and functions of animal and plant tissues (only four types of tissues in animals; Meristematic and Permanent tissues in plants).

Theme: Moving Things, People and Ideas
Unit III: Motion, Force and Work

Chapter – 8 Motion

Motion: Distance and displacement, velocity; uniform and non-uniform motion along a straight line; acceleration, distance-time and velocity-time graphs for uniform motion and uniformly accelerated motion, derivation of equations of motion by graphical method; elementary idea of uniform circular motion.

Chapter – 9 Force and Laws of Motion Force and Newton's laws:

Force and Motion, Newton's Laws of Motion, Action and Reaction forces, Inertia of a body, Inertia and mass, Momentum, Force and Acceleration. Elementary idea of conservation of Momentum.

PRACTICALS

Practicals should be conducted alongside the concepts taught in theory classes.

TERM-I

LIST OF EXPERIMENTS

1.Preparation of:

a) a true solution of common salt, sugar and alum

b) a suspension of soil, chalk powder and fine sand in water

c) a colloidal solution of starch in water and egg albumin/milk in water and distinguish between these on the basis of

• transparency

• filtration criterion

• stability Unit-I: (Chapter -2)

2.Preparation of

a) A mixture

b) A compound

using iron filings and sulphur powder and distinguishing between these on the basis of:

i. appearance, i.e., homogeneity and heterogeneity

ii. behaviour towards a magnet Page 5 of 10

iii. behaviour towards carbon disulphide as a solvent

iv. effect of heat Unit-I:(Chapter-2)

3.Perform the following reactions and classify them as physical or chemical changes

a) Iron with copper sulphate solution in water

b) Burning of magnesium ribbon in air

c) Zinc with dilute sulphuric acid

d) Heating of copper sulphate crystals e) Sodium sulphate with barium chloride in the form of their solutions in water.

Unit-I:(Chapter-2)

4.Preparation of stained temporary mounts of (a) onion peel, (b) human cheek cells & to record observations and draw their labeled diagrams. Unit-II:(Chapter-5)

5.Identification of Parenchyma, Collenchyma and Sclerenchyma tissues in plants, striped, smooth and cardiac muscle fibers and nerve cells in animals, from prepared slides. Draw their labeled diagrams. Unit-II:(Chapter-6)

For Science, students will also be provided with NCERT Exemplar for prescribed extra questions practices.

CHAPTER FOUR

Social Science Syllabus Term I

CBSE Class 9 Social Science Term 1 Syllabus 2022-2023:
  COURSE STRUCTURE

| | | M. MARKS: 40 | |
No.	Units	No. of Periods	Marks
I	India and the Contemporary World -1	17	10
II	Contemporary India – I	14	10
III	Democratic Politics – I	20	10
IV	Economics	20	10
	Total	**71**	**40**

COURSE STRUCTURE TERM I

COURSE CONTENT
Unit 1: India and the Contemporary World – I
Section 1: Events and Processes: (Theme one)
I. The French Revolution
• French Society during the late eighteenth century
• The Outbreak of the Revolution
• France abolishes Monarchy and Becomes a Republic
• Did Women have a Revolution?
• The Abolition of Slavery
• The Revolution and Everyday Life
Unit 2: Contemporary India – I

1. India
• Size and Location
• India and the World
• India's Neighbours
2. Physical Features of India
• Major Physiographic Divisions

Unit 3: Democratic Politics – I
1. What is Democracy? Why Democracy?
• What is Democracy?
• Features of Democracy
• Why Democracy?
• Broader Meaning of Democracy
2. Constitutional Design
• Why do we need a Constitution?
• Making of the Indian Constitution
• Guiding Values of the Indian Constitution

Unit 4: Economics
1. The Story of Village Palampur
• Overview
• Organization of production
• Farming in Palampur
• Non-farm activities of Palampur
2. People as Resource
• Overview
• Economic activities by men and women
• Quality of Population
• Unemployment

List of Map Items for Term – I
SUBJECT - HISTORY
Chapter-1: The French Revolution
Outline Political Map of France
Bordeaux
Nantes
Paris
Marseilles

SUBJECT – GEOGRAPHY

Chapter -1: India-Size and Location

India-States with Capitals, Tropic of Cancer, Standard Meridian

Chapter -2: Physical Features of India

Mountain Ranges: The Karakoram, The Zasker, The Shivalik, The Aravali, The Vindhya, The Satpura, Western & Eastern Ghats

Mountain Peaks: K2, Kanchan Junga, Anai Mudi

Plateau: Deccan Plateau, Chotta Nagpur Plateau, Malwa Plateau

Coastal Plains: Konkan, Malabar, Coromandel & Northern Circar

	Marks	Description	
Periodic Assessment	10 Marks	Pen Paper Test	5 marks
		Assessment using multiple strategies For example, Quiz, Debate, Role Play, Viva, Group Discussion, Visual Expression, Interactive Bulletin Boards, Gallery Walks, Exit Cards, Concept Maps, Peer Assessment, Self-Assessment, etc.	5 marks
Portfolio	5 Marks	• Classwork and Assignments • Any exemplary work done by the student • Reflections, Narrations, Journals, etc. • Achievements of the student in the subject throughout the year • Participation of the student in different activities like Heritage India Quiz	
Subject Enrichment Activity	5 Marks	• Project Work	
TOTAL	**20 MARKS**		

INTERNAL ASSESSMENT TERM I

PROJECT WORK

1. Every student has to compulsorily undertake one project on Disaster Management.

2. Objectives: The main objectives of giving project work on Disaster Management to the students are to:

a. create awareness in them about different disasters, their consequences and management

b. prepare them in advance to face such situations

c. ensure their participation in disaster mitigation plans

d. enable them to create awareness and preparedness among the community.

3. The project work should also help in enhancing the Life Skills of the students.

4. If possible, different forms of art may be integrated in the project work.

5. In order to realize the expected objectives completely, it would be required of the Principals / Teachers to muster support from various local authorities and organizations like the Disaster Management Authorities, Relief, Rehabilitation and the Disaster Management Departments of the States, Office of the District Magistrate/ Deputy Commissioners, Fire Service, Police, Civil Defense etc. in the area where the schools are located.

6. The distribution of marks over different aspects relating to Project Work is asfollows:

S. No.	Aspects	Marks
a.	Content accuracy, originality and analysis	2
b.	Presentation and creativity	2
c.	Viva Voce	1

PROJECT ASSESSMENT PATTERN

7. The project carried out by the students should subsequently be shared among themselves through interactive sessions such as exhibitions, panel discussions, etc.

8. All documents pertaining to assessment under this activity should be meticulously maintained by the schools.

9. A Summary Report should be prepared highlighting:

a. objectives realized through individual work and group interactions

b. calendar of activities

c. innovative ideas generated in the process (like comic strips, drawings, illustrations, script play etc.);

d. list of questions asked in viva voce.

10. It is to be noted here by all the teachers and students that the projects and models prepared should be made from eco-friendly products without incurring too much expenditure.

11. The Project Report should be handwritten by the students themselves.

12. The record of the project work (internal assessment) should be kept for a period of three months for verification, if any.

CHAPTER FIVE

English Syllabus Term II

Course Structure for CBSE Class 9 English (Code No. 184) 2021-2022 (Term II):

SECTION	WEIGHTAGE (IN MARKS)
READING	10
WRITING & GRAMMAR	10
LITERATURE	20
TOTAL	40
INTERNAL ASSESSMENT	10
GRAND TOTAL	50

Pattern for Term 1 and Term 2

Reading-

Question based on the following kinds of unseen passages to assess inference, evaluation, vocabulary, analysis and interpretation:

1. Discursive passage (400-450 words)

2. Case based Factual passage (with visual input/ statistical data/ chart etc. 200-250 words)

Writing

1. Descriptive Paragraph (Diary)

2. Story writing (based on beginning line, outline, cues etc.)

Grammar

1. Tenses

2. Subject-Verb Concord

3. Modals

4. Determiners

5. Reported Speech

6. Commands and Requests

7. Statements

8. Questions

Literature

Questions based on extracts / texts to assess interpretation, inference, extrapolation beyond the text and across the texts.

Moments

1. Weathering the Storm in Ersama

2. The Last Leaf

3. A House is not a Home

4. The Beggar

Beehive

Prose

1. Packing

2. Reach for The Top

3. The Bond of Love

4. If I were You

Poems

1. No Men Are Foreign

2. On killing a Tree

3. The Snake Trying

CHAPTER SIX

Mathematics Syllabus Term II

COURSE STRUCTURE CLASS –IX (2021-22) SECOND TERM

No.	Unit Name	Marks
I	Algebra (Cont.)	12
II	Geometry (Cont.)	15
III	Mensuration (Cont.)	9
IV	Statistics & Probability (Cont)	4
IV	Total	40
	Internal Assessment	10
	Total	50

Pattern For Term 1I

UNIT-ALGEBRA

1.POLYNOMIALS

Definition of a polynomial in one variable, with examples and counter examples. Coefficients of a polynomial, terms of a polynomial and zero polynomial. Degree of a polynomial. Constant, linear, quadratic and cubic polynomials. Monomials, binomials, trinomials. Factors and multiples. Zeros of a polynomial. Factorization of $ax2 + bx + c$, $a \neq 0$ where a, b and c are real numbers, and of cubic polynomials using the Factor Theorem.

UNIT-GEOMETRY

2.QUADRILATERALS

(Prove) The diagonal divides a parallelogram into two congruent triangles.

(Motivate) In a parallelogram opposite sides are equal, and conversely.

(Motivate) In a parallelogram opposite angles are equal, and conversely.

(Motivate) A quadrilateral is a parallelogram if a pair of its opposite sides is parallel and equal.

(Motivate) In a parallelogram, the diagonals bisect each other and conversely.

(Motivate) In a triangle, the line segment joining the mid points of any two sides is parallel to the third side and in half of it and (motivate) its converse.

3.CIRCLES

Through examples, arrive at definition of circle and related concepts-radius, circumference, diameter, chord, arc, secant, sector, segment, subtended angle.

(Prove) Equal chords of a circle subtend equal angles at the centre and (motivate) its converse.

(Motivate) The perpendicular from the centre of a circle to a chord bisects the chord and conversely, the line drawn through the centre of a circle to bisect a chord is perpendicular to the chord.

(Motivate) Equal chords of a circle (or of congruent circles) are equidistant from the centre (or their respective centres) and conversely.

(Motivate) The angle subtended by an arc at the centre is double the angle subtended by it at any point on the remaining part of the circle.

(Motivate) Angles in the same segment of a circle are equal.

(Motivate) The sum of either of the pair of the opposite angles of a cyclic quadrilateral is 180° and its converse.

4.CONSTRUCTIONS

Construction of bisectors of line segments and angles of measure 60°, 90°, 45° etc., equilateral triangles.

Construction of a triangle given its base, sum/difference of the other two sides and one base angle.

UNIT-MENSURATION

5.SURFACE AREAS AND VOLUMES

Surface areas and volumes of cubes, cuboids, spheres (including hemispheres) and right circular cylinders/cones.

UNIT-STATISTICS & PROBABILITY

6.PROBABILITY

History, Repeated experiments and observed frequency approach to probability. Focus is on empirical probability. (A large amount of time to be devoted to group and to individual activities to motivate the concept; the experiments to be drawn from real - life situations, and from examples used in the chapter on statistics).

INTERNAL ASSESSMENT	MARKS	Total MARKS
Periodic Tests	3	
Multiple Assessments	2	
		10 marks for the term
Portfolio	2	
Student Enrichment Activities-practical work	3	

Internal Assessment Term II

For Mathematics, students will also be provided with NCERT Exemplar for prescribed extra questions practices.

• 21 •

CHAPTER SEVEN

Science Syllabus Term II

CBSE Class 9 Science (Subject Code - 086) Syllabus 2021-22 (Term 2)

Units	Term-II	Marks
I	Matter-Its Nature and Behaviour: Chapter 3 and 4	18
II	Organization in the Living World: Chapter - 13	08
III	Motion, Force and Work: Chapter - 10 and 11	14
	Total	40
	Internal Assessment	10
	Total	50

Assessment Pattern Term II

TERM – II
Theme: Materials
Unit I: Matter- It's Nature and Behaviour
Chapter – 3 Atoms and Molecules

Particle nature and their basic units: Atoms and molecules, Law of constant proportions, Atomic and molecular masses. Mole concept: Relationship of mole to mass of the particles and numbers.

Chapter – 4 Structure of Atom

Structure of atoms: Electrons, protons and neutrons, valency, chemical formula of common compounds. Isotopes and Isobars.

Theme: Moving Things, People and Ideas

Unit III: Motion, Force and Work

Chapter – 10 Gravitation

Gravitation: Gravitation; Universal Law of Gravitation, Force of Gravitation of the earth (gravity), Acceleration due to Gravity; Mass and Weight; Free fall.

Chapter – 11 Work and Energy

Work, energy and power: Work done by a Force, Energy, power; Kinetic and Potential energy; Law of conservation of energy

Theme: The World of the Living

Unit II: Organization in the Living World

Chapter – 13 Why do we fall ill

Health and Diseases: Health and its failure. Infectious and Non-infectious diseases, their causes and manifestation.Diseases caused by microbes (Virus, Bacteria and Protozoans) and their prevention; Principles of treatment and prevention. Pulse Polio programmes.

ONLY FOR INTERNAL ASSESSMENT

Note: Learners are assigned to read the below listed part of Unit IV. They can be encouraged to prepare a brief write up on any one concept of this Unit in their Portfolio. This may be an assessment for Internal Assessment and credit may be given (Periodic assessment/Portfolio). This portion of the Unit is not to be assessed in the year-end examination.

Theme: Natural Resources: Balance in nature

Unit IV: Our Environment

Chapter -14 Natural Resources

Physical resources: Air, Water, Soil. Air for respiration, for combustion, for moderating temperatures; movements of air and its role in bringing rains across India.

Air, water and soil pollution (brief introduction).Holes in ozone layer and the probable damages.

Bio-geo chemical cycles in nature: Water, Oxygen, Carbon and Nitrogen.

PRACTICALS

Practicals should be conducted alongside the concepts taught in theory classes.

TERM-II

LIST OF EXPERIMENTS

1. Determination of the density of solid (denser than water) by using a spring balance and a measuring cylinder. Unit-III:(Chapter–10)

2. Establishing the relation between the loss in weight of a solid when fully immersed in

a) Tap water

b) Strongly salty water with the weight of water displaced by it by taking at least two different solids. Unit-III:(Chapter–10)

3. Verification of the law of conservation of mass in a chemical reaction. Unit-I:(Chapter–3)

For Science, students will also be provided with NCERT Exemplar for prescribed extra questions practices.

CHAPTER EIGHT

Social Science Syllabus Term II

CBSE Class 9 Social Science Term 1 Syllabus 2022-2023:
   Course Structure

			M. MARKS: 40
No.	**Units**	**No. of Periods**	**Marks**
I	India and the Contemporary World -1	34	10
II	Contemporary India – I	24	10
III	Democratic Politics – I	18	10
IV	Economics	10	10
	Total	**86**	**40**

COURSE STRUCTURE TERM II

Course Content Class 9th Term 2

Unit 1: India and the Contemporary World – I

Section 1: Events and Processes: (Theme two and three)

II. Socialism in Europe and the Russian Revolution

• The Age of Social Change

• The Russian Revolution

• The February Revolution in Petrograd

• What Changed after October?

• The Global Influence of the Russian Revolution and the USSR

III. Nazism and the Rise of Hitler

• Birth of the Weimar Republic

- Hitler's Rise to Power
- The Nazi Worldview
- Youth in Nazi Germany
- Ordinary People and the Crimes Against Humanity

Unit 2: Contemporary India – I

3. Drainage
- Major rivers and tributaries
- Lakes
- Role of rivers in the economy
- Pollution of rivers

Note: Only Map Items as given in the Map List from this chapter to be evaluated in Examination.

4. Climate
- Concept
- Climatic Controls
- Factors influencing India's climate
- The Indian Monsoon
- Distribution of Rainfall
- Monsoon as a unifying bond

5. Natural Vegetation and Wild Life
- Factors affecting Vegetation
- Vegetation types
- Wild Life Conservation

Unit 3: Democratic Politics – I

3. Electoral Politics
- Why Elections?
- What is our System of Elections?
- What makes elections in India democratic?

4. Working of Institutions
- How is the major policy decision taken?
- Parliament
- Political Executive
- Judiciary

Unit 4: Economics

3. Poverty as a Challenge

• Two typical cases of poverty
• Poverty as seen by Social Scientists
• Poverty Estimates
• Vulnerable Groups
• Interstate disparities
• Global Poverty Scenario
• Causes of Poverty
• Anti-poverty measures
• The Challenges Ahead

List of Map Items Class 9 Term 2

SUBJECT - HISTORY

Chapter-2: Socialism in Europe and the Russian Revolution

Outline Political Map of World (For locating and labeling / Identification)

Major countries of First World War

(Central Powers and Allied Powers)

Central Powers - Germany, Austria-Hungary, Turkey (Ottoman Empire)

Allied Powers - France, England, Russia, U.S.A.

Chapter-3: Nazism and Rise of Hitler

Outline Political Map of World (For locating and labeling / Identification)

Major countries of Second World War

Axis Powers – Germany, Italy, Japan

Allied Powers – UK, France, Former USSR, USA

Territories under German expansion (Nazi Power) Austria, Poland, Czechoslovakia (only Slovakia shown in the map), Denmark, Lithuania, France, Belgium

SUBJECT – GEOGRAPHY

(Outline Political Map of India)

Chapter -3: Drainage

Rivers: (Identification only)

o The Himalayan River Systems-The Indus, The Ganges, and The Satluj o The Peninsular rivers-The Narmada, The Tapi, The Kaveri, The Krishna, The Godavari, The Mahanadi

Lakes: Wular, Pulicat, Sambhar, Chilika

Chapter - 4: Climate

Areas receiving rainfall less than 20 cm and over 400 cm (Identification only)

Chapter - 5: Natural Vegetation and Wild Life

Vegetation Type: Tropical Evergreen Forest, Tropical Deciduous Forest, Thorn Forest, Montane Forests and Mangrove- For identification only

National Parks: Corbett, Kaziranga, Ranthambor, Shivpuri, Kanha, Simlipal & Manas

Bird Sanctuaries: Bharatpur and Ranganthitto

Wild Life Sanctuaries: Sariska, Mudumalai, Rajaji, Dachigam (Location and Labelling)

Internal Assessment

Project Work:

1. Every student has to compulsorily undertake one project on Disaster Management.

2. Objectives: The main objectives of giving project work on Disaster Management to the students are to:

a. create awareness in them about different disasters, their consequences and management

b. prepare them in advance to face such situations

c. ensure their participation in disaster mitigation plans

d. enable them to create awareness and preparedness among the community.

3. The project work should also help in enhancing the Life Skills of the students.

4. If possible, different forms of art may be integrated in the project work.

5. In order to realize the expected objectives completely, it would be required of the Principals / Teachers to muster support from various local authorities and organizations like the Disaster Management Authorities, Relief, Rehabilitation and the Disaster

Management Departments of the States, Office of the District Magistrate/ Deputy Commissioners, Fire Service, Police, Civil Defense etc. in the area where the schools are located.

6. The distribution of marks over different aspects relating to Project Work is same as for Term I.

7. The project carried out by the students should subsequently be shared among themselves through interactive sessions such as exhibitions, panel discussions, etc.

8. All documents pertaining to assessment under this activity should be meticulously maintained by the schools.

9. A Summary Report should be prepared highlighting:

a. objectives realized through individual work and group interactions

b. calendar of activities

c. innovative ideas generated in the process (like comic strips, drawings, illustrations, script play etc.);

d. list of questions asked in viva voce.

10. It is to be noted here by all the teachers and students that the projects and models prepared should be made from eco-friendly products without incurring too much expenditure.

11. The Project Report should be handwritten by the students themselves.

12. The record of the project work (internal assessment) should be kept for a period of three months for verification, if any.

CHAPTER NINE

Overall View

Total Number of Lessons to be studied in the Academic Year 2022-23

Subject	Total Lessons
English	21
Mathematics	15
Science	15
Social Science	20
Total Lessons	**71**
Excluding Grammar and Writing Skills for English. They will be taught but is not included in this count.	

Total Number of Month wise Working Days

Month	Working Days	Total Weekend Test
April	26	4
May	Complete Off	
June	26	4
July	26	5
August	26	4
September	26	4
October	22	4
November	26	4
December	25	4
January	25	5
February	24	4
March	Final Examination Revision	
Total	254	42

List of Holidays:

15th August: Independence Day

22nd October to 26th October: Diwali Vacations

26th January: Republic Day

Class Duration: 2 Hours Per Day

Timings will be decided with your consent.

Note that there are many tests planned based on JEE | NEET Pattern as well. All Month End Tests will follow JEE | NEET | MH-CET Test Patterns.

First Weekend MCQ Tests will be conducted online on Heavenly Blessings Mobile Application to provide the practise of CPT pattern.

Second Weekend MCQ Test will be conducted offline.

Third Weekend MCQ Test will be conducted online on Heavenly Blessings Mobile Application based on JEE | NEET | MH-CET Pattern.

Fourth Weekend Test will be a subjective test. Subject will be informed timely.